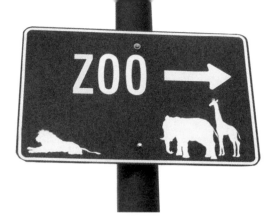

Learning to Read, Step by Step!

Ready to Read Preschool–Kindergarten
• big type and easy words • rhyme and rhythm • picture clues
For children who know the alphabet and are eager to
begin reading.

Reading with Help Preschool–Grade 1
• basic vocabulary • short sentences • simple stories
For children who recognize familiar words and sound out
new words with help.

Reading on Your Own Grades 1–3
• engaging characters • easy-to-follow plots • popular topics
For children who are ready to read on their own.

Reading Paragraphs Grades 2–3
• challenging vocabulary • short paragraphs • exciting stories
For newly independent readers who read simple sentences
with confidence.

Ready for Chapters Grades 2–4
• chapters • longer paragraphs • full-color art
For children who want to take the plunge into chapter books
but still like colorful pictures.

STEP INTO READING® is designed to give every child a successful
reading experience. The grade levels are only guides; children will progress
through the steps at their own speed, developing confidence in their reading.
The F&P Text Level on the back cover serves as another tool to help you
choose the right book for your child.

Remember, a lifetime love of reading starts with a single step!

For Cooper and Chase
Love, Granola

Copyright © 2014 by Sherry Shahan

All rights reserved. Published in the United States by Random House Children's Books, a division of Random House LLC, a Penguin Random House Company, New York. This work is based on *Feeding Time at the Zoo,* copyright © 2000 by Sherry Shahan, published in paperback by Random House Children's Books, New York, in 2000.

Step into Reading, Random House, and the Random House colophon are registered trademarks of Random House LLC.

Visit us on the Web!
StepIntoReading.com
randomhouse.com/kids

Educators and librarians, for a variety of teaching tools, visit us at
RHTeachersLibrarians.com

Library of Congress Cataloging-in-Publication Data
Shahan, Sherry.
Feeding time at the zoo / by Sherry Shahan.
   pages   cm. — (Step into reading)
ISBN 978-0-385-37190-2 (trade) — ISBN 978-0-375-97190-7 (lib. bdg.) —
ISBN 978-0-375-98177-7 (ebook)
1. Zoo animals—Food—Juvenile literature. 2. Zoo animals—Feeding and feeds—Juvenile literature. I. Title.
QL77.5.S46 2014   591.5'3—dc23   2013031327

Printed in the United States of America
10 9 8 7 6 5 4 3 2 1

This book has been officially leveled by using the F&P Text Level Gradient™ Leveling System.

Feeding Time
at the ZOO

by Sherry Shahan

Random House New York

It is feeding time at the zoo.

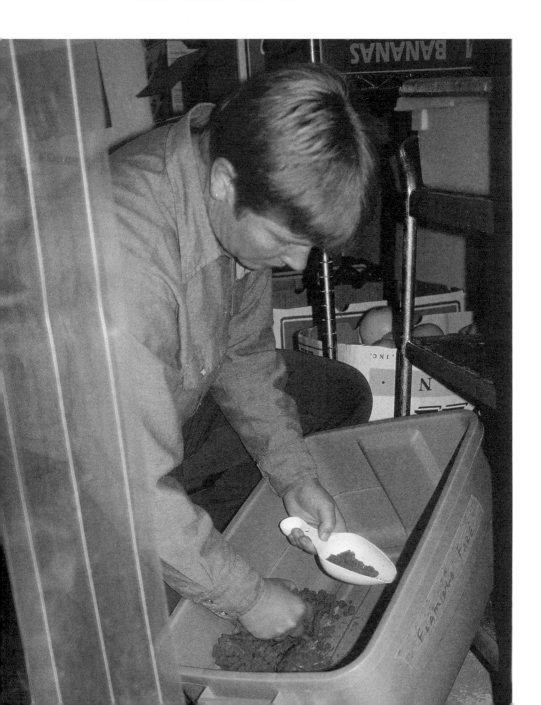

Chop! Chop! Chop!
A zookeeper
chops up food.

The food goes onto
a cart.

What do zoo animals eat?

This elephant loves watermelon!

Elephants also eat hay.

Zebras eat hay
and other plant foods.

So do giraffes,
with a long drink
of water!

The panda bear eats
bamboo leaves.
Bamboo grows
at the zoo.

Pigs munch salad.

They eat corn too.

Even the corncobs!

Crunch!

Tortoises like veggies.

Do you?

How about fruit?

Porcupines eat veggies and fruit.
This porcupine nibbles a yummy banana.

Tigers eat meat.
This big guy eats
a big meatball.

Then he naps in the sun.

Alligators eat meat too.

The zookeeper feeds
this one
with a broom!

Chomp!

A sea lion barks for fish.
Arf! Arf! Arf!

Polar bears eat fish too!

The macaw
peels an orange
with his beak.

A cockatoo likes carrots.

Both birds eat seeds.

Flamingos scoop up
tiny shrimp.
The shrimp are pink.

That is why flamingos
are pink.

A girl holds an
ice cream cone.

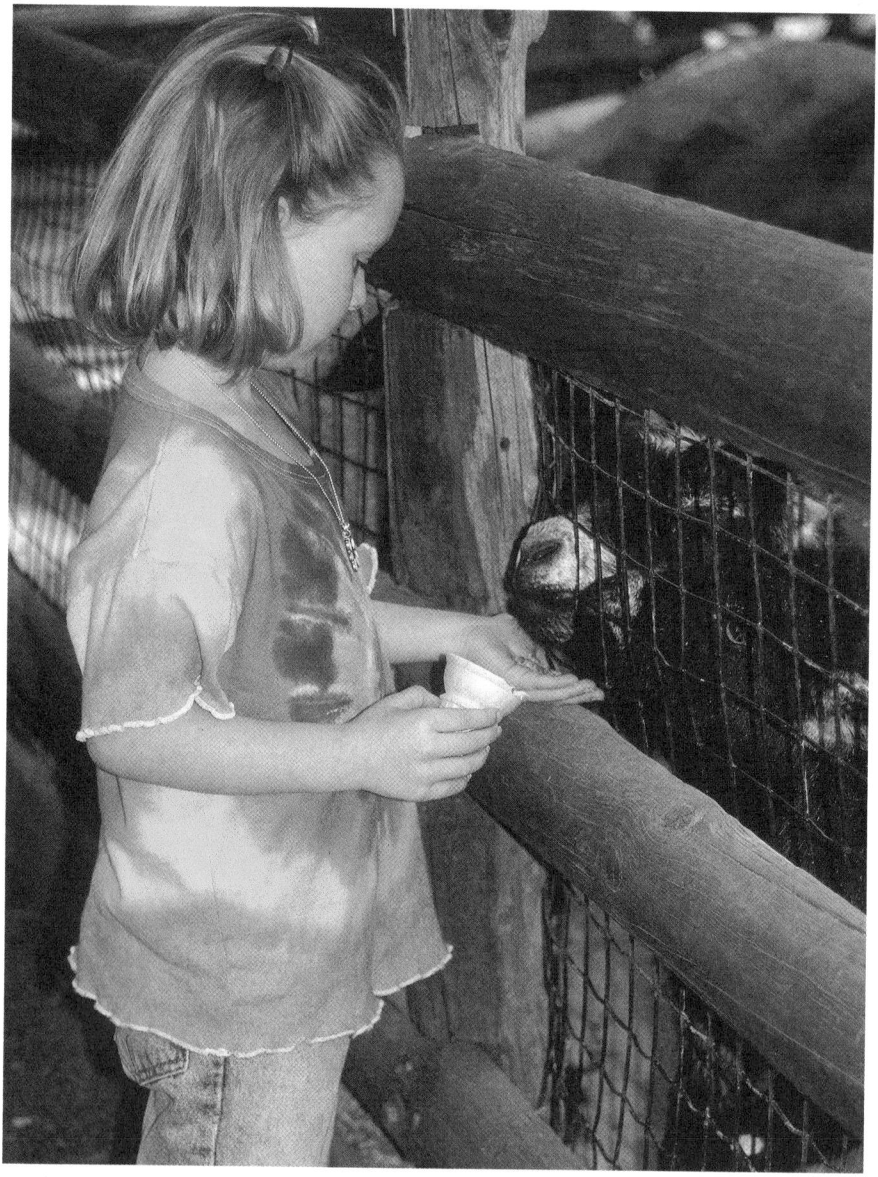

Inside are food pellets
for the animals.

Animals love
these snacks!

You can feed a goat.

Or pet it!

What do kids eat
at the zoo?

Hay?

Bamboo?

Corncobs?

No! Ice pops!